Technology All Around Us

Robots

Clive Gifford

W
FRANKLIN WATTS
LONDON•SYDNEY

First published in 2005 by
Franklin Watts
96 Leonard Street
London EC2A 4XD

Franklin Watts Australia
Level 17/207 Kent Street
Sydney
NSW 2000

Produced by Arcturus Publishing Ltd,
26/27 Bickels Yard, 151-153 Bermondsey Street, London SE1
3HA

© 2005 Arcturus Publishing

Series concept: Alex Woolf
Editor: Alex Woolf
Designer: Simon Borrough
Picture researcher: Glass Onion Pictures

Picture Credits
Science Photo Library: 4 (Peter Menzel), 5 (Peter Menzel), 6
(Sheila Terry), 7 (Maximilian Stock Ltd), 8 and cover (Sam
Ogden), 9 (Peter Menzel), 10 (NASA / Carnegie Mellon
University), 11 (Peter Menzel), 12 (James King-Holmes), 13
(Peter Menzel), 14 (Peter Menzel), 15 (Pascal Goetgheluck), 16
(Alexis Rosenfeld), 17 (Peter Menzel), 18 (Alexis Rosenfeld), 19
(Peter Menzel), 20 (NASA), 21 (NASA), 22 (Peter Yates), 23
(Peter Menzel), 24 (Philippe Psaila), 25 (Lawrence Livermore
National Laboratory), 26 (Peter Menzel), 27 (Peter Menzel), 28
(Victor Habbick Visions), 29 (Eye of Science).

Every attempt has been made to clear copyright. Should there
be any inadvertent omission, please apply to the publisher for
rectification.

A CIP catalogue record for this book is available from the British
Library

ISBN 0 7496 5959 9

Printed in Singapore

Contents

What Makes a Robot?

Robots are an exciting and useful type of machine. Their impact on our world is on the increase. Robots can perform a range of helpful tasks with little or no supervision by people.

Those that can work completely by themselves are called autonomous. Others are remote controlled by humans and are called teleoperated machines.

A researcher experiments with Genghis, a robot insect able to make simple decisions and respond to its environment.

Under Orders

Robots follow sets of instructions, usually written as computer programs. Many robots can have their programs changed in order to perform different tasks.

The Cye home robot, for example, can fetch and carry items, act as a home security guard or vacuum a room using different programs and attachments.

>> Looking Forward

The Thinking Robot
Robots can react to their environment and remember things. But their brains are nowhere near as flexible or powerful as the human brain. The goal of many people working in the field of artificial intelligence (AI) is to change that. Already, robots that can learn from their mistakes have been created.

Sensors And Controllers

To work on their own, robots need to know information about themselves and the world around them. Devices called sensors collect information, such as the robot's position or the size of an obstacle ahead.

Sensors pass this data back to a robot's controller. This is the "brain" of the robot, which makes decisions and instructs a robot's parts. The controller is usually some form of computer microprocessor.

The Honda P3 is a humanoid robot (see pages 8–9) capable of walking around obstacles in its path as well as climbing down a flight of stairs without losing its balance.

Degrees Of Freedom

The moving parts of a robot are powered by actuators. These can be electric motors, hydraulic pistons or compressed air systems.

Each direction in which a robot, or a robot part, can move is called a degree of freedom. Robot arms, for instance, are fitted with joints. Each joint may give a robot an extra degree of freedom.

Looking Back

What's In A Name? The word *robot* comes from the Czech word *robota*, meaning "forced labour". It was first used by Czech playwright Karel Capek in his 1920 play *Rossum's Universal Robots*.

His play was about human-like robots that took over the world. This view of robots and their threat to people has remained a popular theme in sci-fi books and films ever since.

More than a million robots are at work today. Almost three-quarters of these are found in industry. There they perform tasks such as welding, spray painting, handling or sorting materials, and transporting items around a factory.

Never tiring or complaining, robots tend to perform jobs that are difficult, unpleasant or tedious for people. They also perform work beyond people's abilities, such as handling red-hot metal or drilling hundreds of small holes with perfect precision.

A pair of industrial AGVs transport barrels of oil around a factory floor without a human in sight.

Technology in Action

Skywash

It is 1996 and staff at German airline Lufthansa look on in awe as a monstrous machine cleans airliners in record time. Called the Skywash SW33, the giant robot arm measures thirty-three metres in length and weighs over twenty tonnes.

When it is cleaning a Boeing 747 jumbo jet, its brushes travel 3.8 kilometres. Traditional cleaning takes nine hours, but with Skywash the job is done in just three and a half hours and uses half the water.

Automated Guided Vehicles (AGVs)

AGVs are mobile robots that work mainly in factories, but also in hospitals and offices. They ferry materials, supplies and equipment around the workplace without a human driver.

Many of these wheeled machines use light sensors to follow a bright line on the building floor to plot a safe route.

Looking Back

The First Industrial Robot George Devol and Joseph Engelberger met at a party in 1956 and discussed sci-fi books and movies. Within five years, the pair had turned science fiction into fact with the world's very first industrial robot, called the Unimate I.

This four-tonne robot was employed at a General Motors car factory in the United States. Obeying step-by-step instructions recorded on a magnetic drum, the robot handled hot metal castings slowly but surely.

Demolition Robots

Robots are used in demolition, particularly in tight spaces where high dust levels and falling material could harm human workers.

The Brokk 40 robot arm can be fitted with tile chiselling and concrete crushing tools. It can perform demolition work four times faster than a human team of workers.

A robot arm guides a welding torch into perfect position. It is directed with unerring accuracy by a system of lasers and miniature cameras.

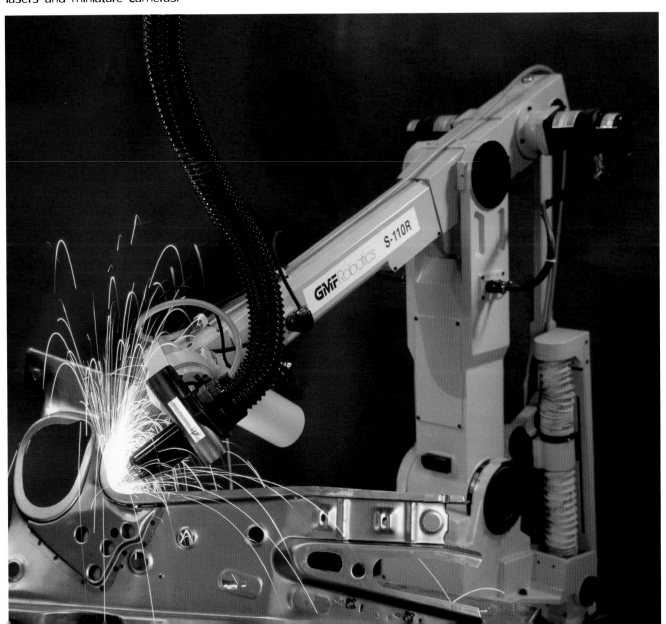

7

For centuries, people have been fascinated by the idea of creating machines that look and act like themselves. Mechanical models of people, moved by clockwork, appeared in medieval clocks and are called automata.

Today, humanoid robots look and act like people. They are also capable of reacting to their environment and making decisions.

Looking Forward

Giving Robots Personality Robotics teams in many countries are seeking to build robots that can display emotions and learn to develop their own personalities.

In the USA, a robot baby called Robota is being built that watches human actions and learns to imitate them in order to build up different ways of acting.

Another robot called Kismet is able to show a range of emotions. It shows emotions as different facial expressions, using actuators to move parts of its face.

Robotics researcher Cynthia Breazeal "plays" with Kismet. This robot has been equipped with sensors and software which simulate the behaviour of a baby or young child.

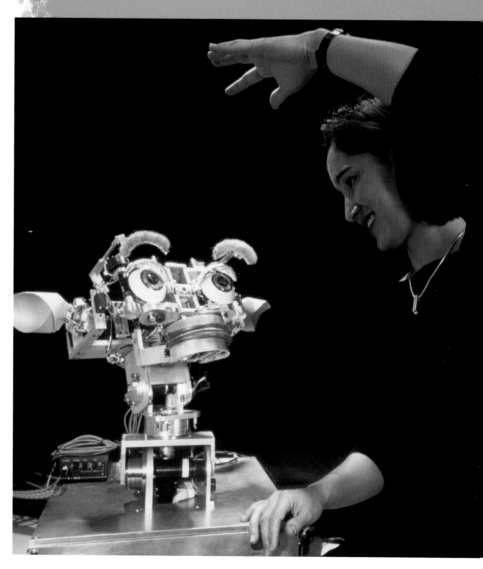

Balancing Bipeds

Early biped (two-legged) robots struggled to keep their balance, especially when walking. They did not have the sophisticated balancing system found in the human ear and brain.

Advances in robotics have led to robots, such as the Honda Asimo, being able to walk and even climb stairs.

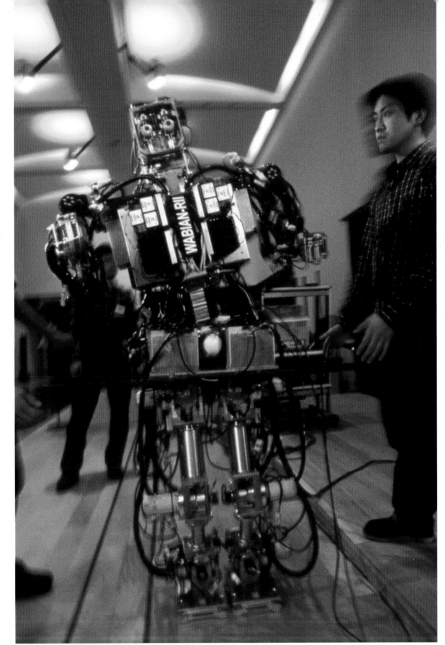

Researchers look on as Waseda University's WABIAN II humanoid robot walks through a Japanese laboratory.

Sony Qrio

The Sony Qrio is a humanoid robot, just fifty-eight centimetres tall, that can walk, dance and speak a vocabulary of 60,000 words. Using microphones and digital cameras, the Qrio can recognize voices and faces and read emails and Web pages.

Gripping Stuff

Some humanoid robots strive to equal human's amazing ability to hold and manipulate objects of different sizes, shapes and weights.

COG, for example, has four-fingered hands covered in a touch-sensitive material. The fingers can tell the robot what sort of material they are gripping. The robot can adjust the force of their grip to prevent an object slipping. It can also release some pressure to prevent damage to the object.

Looking Back

Made In Japan Between 1980 and 1984, Waseda University developed a pioneering humanoid robot called WABOT-2. Although it could not balance or walk, WABOT-2 still wowed the world with its impressive musical abilities.

The robot's cameras and controller enabled WABOT-2 to read a piece of sheet music and play the music on an electric organ with its two robot hands.

Robots can explore places where people cannot or dare not go. These include places too far away or simply too dangerous for people to reach.

Robot explorers don't need to carry food, water and other supplies. Energy to power their parts can come from batteries or solar panels. Robots can be built with their electronic components protected so that they can work in boiling hot or freezing cold environments.

Looking Back

The Inferno In July 1994, an eight-legged robot called Dante II climbed slowly into the mouth of an active volcanic crater on Mount Spurr, Alaska. Despite being hit by a boulder which damaged one of its legs, Dante II managed to reach the crater floor.

It collected video footage using its eight cameras and took samples of gases and water found in the crater. But a fall ended the robot's mission and it had to be airlifted out by helicopter.

Dante II in action exploring Mount Spurr. The robot was equipped with sensors that measured the sorts of gases found in the volcano.

Professor William "Red" Whittaker with Nomad. The robot has trekked in the hot, dry deserts of Chile as well as freezing Antarctica.

Exploring Ancient Egypt

Robots can explore cramped environments too small for humans to enter. In 2002, iRobot's Pyramid Rover travelled down a shaft just twenty centimetres high and twenty centimetres wide. The robot explored a place unseen by modern eyes – inside the 4,500-year-old ancient Egyptian Great Pyramid.

Industrial Explorers

Many robot explorers don't make the headlines but perform valuable work in industry. Long, narrow, snake-like robots, made up of lots of flexible sections, are sent down pipelines and sewer systems. They are used to check for leaks and other problems.

Other robots equipped with sniffing sensors can enter storage tanks to hunt out gas leaks.

Technology in Action

Meteorite Hunter
It is January 2000. The location is the icy wastes of Antarctica where the sub-zero temperatures would kill a person in a matter of hours. A chunky robot rover, almost the size of a Volkswagen Beetle car, is hunting for meteorites. Its name is Nomad.

Nomad covers an area of 2,500 square metres over ten days. It uses cameras and sensors to examine a hundred different rocks. On 22 January, Nomad discovers a meteorite, the first of five that the robot finds.

Service robots perform a range of dull, repetitive but useful tasks. Some can fill a car's petrol tank, whilst others carry a golfer's bag of clubs. In Japan, a robot shopping trolley follows a customer obediently around a department store.

Service robots are in their infancy, but many more are expected to appear in the near future.

The Hefter Robot Cleaner in action in Manchester Airport, England. The robot is guided by ultrasound sensors and lasers to avoid colliding with objects, and issues a spoken message if people get in the way.

Clean Machine
Cleaning robots are used to scrub the floors in several British hospitals, on the Paris Metro and at a number of airports in Asia. Climbing robots, designed in France and Germany, have scaled the sides of skyscrapers, cleaning windows.

Looking Forward:

Robo-gardeners Delicate seedlings can now be repotted using special robot arms. Robot lawnmowers are already on sale to the public. Robots used to hunt down garden pests may also soon be a reality.

Slugbot is a small, four-wheeled prototype robot. It can capture a hundred slugs per hour with its three-fingered claw. The slugs rot in a special refuelling chamber. Gases from the rotting slugs are converted into electricity to power the robot.

Served By Service Bots

Robot waiters and bartenders are becoming a reality. In Yo Sushi restaurants in Europe, AGV robots (see page 6) move between tables carrying drinks to customers.

Cynthia is a resident bartender in London's Wicked Bar and Restaurant. She is a two-metre-tall humanoid robot with two gripping arms which help her serve one of seventy-five different cocktails.

This prototype German robot can fill a motor vehicle's tank with petrol with no supervision required.

Meet Minerva

It is 1998 and visitors arrive at the National Museum of American History in Washington DC. A squat, grey machine glides over to meet the visitors, welcoming them with some words spoken in a soft, human-like voice.

The robot is called Minerva and it guides visitors through the Material World exhibition at the museum. The robot plots it own path through the exhibition, speaking, singing and answering questions via its touchscreen.

Get in its way once and the robot stops and says, "excuse me" in polite tones. Get in its way repeatedly and expect to get a blast of its horn and see its face form a frown.

Rescue Robots

Robots can save lives. They can enter disaster zones or dangerous areas, seeking out victims or trying to stop a fire or chemical leak. Robots also perform the nuclear power industry's dirty work, helping to dismantle damaged nuclear power plants.

In the future, large groups of small, highly mobile machines may work together. Called a robot swarm, these robots would scour an area, searching for disaster victims.

Looking Forward

Treating Trapped Survivors The Center for Robot Assisted Search and Rescue (CRASAR) is building robots that can squeeze their way through a disaster site and reach trapped victims.

The robots will perform a medical diagnosis on patients, checking their vital signs. They will also bring the survivors water, oxygen and basic medical supplies. The robots' radios will provide a communications link between the victims and the rescue forces.

The Japanese Blue Dragon robot crawls over a pile of rubble using a nose-mounted digital camera to "see" what lies in its path.

Firefighters

Firefighting robots are on trial with many emergency services. They can handle heat from a blaze better than human firefighters. They can also remain unaffected by lethal, poisonous smoke. Some can use regular firefighting tools such as hoses and extinguishers.

Expendable Machines

Robots are used to detect mines or handle unexploded bombs without putting people at risk. Bomb-disposal robots usually move on wheels or tracks and are equipped with a robot arm. Different tools can be fitted to the arm. Sharp steel probes can be used to break windows. Grippers and claws can manipulate suspicious packages.

Some bomb-disposal robots are fitted with disrupters. These fire a powerful jet of water into a bomb to break up its circuits before the bomb can explode.

Bomb Disposal in Israel
It is 2002 and the police are called to a bus-stop near the Israeli city of Haifa. There are fears that an unconscious man is a suicide bomber carrying deadly explosives on his body.

The police deploy a tracked bomb-disposal robot. Controlled from a safe distance, the robot uses its manipulator arm to turn the man over. Cameras and sensors send data back to the bomb-disposal team. Finally, the all clear is given, thanks to the robot.

A tracked bomb-disposal robot manoeuvres a water-cannon disrupter into position to disarm the circuits of a car bomb.

Flying Robots

Most robots are fairly slow moving on land or in water. Flying robots, known as Unmanned Aerial Vehicles (UAVs), have to travel more rapidly. This is so that their wings move through the air fast enough to create the lift needed to keep them airborne. Because of their high speed, almost all UAVs are remote-controlled.

This unmanned aircraft is being prepared for flight. It will act as a flying target to test the accuracy of missiles at a French missile-testing centre.

Round-the-World Robot

In April 2001, an aircraft unlike any other flew across the Pacific Ocean from the United States to Australia. The machine had a wingspan of thirty-five metres, and was called *Global Hawk*. It was an unmanned aerial vehicle and the first flying robot to cross the Pacific.

Flying non-stop for twenty-three hours and twenty minutes, the robot completed its 13,000-kilometre trip without a hitch. On later flights it broke the altitude and endurance world records for flying robots.

Spies in the Sky

A number of unmanned aerial vehicles are being used as spies in the sky. Equipped with powerful zoom cameras, these robots can fly over enemy territory. Some fly at very high altitudes to avoid enemy aircraft. Others fly below enemy radar at ground-hugging low altitudes.

One unusual flying spy is Cypher. This doughnut-shaped machine has its helicopter-style blades spinning inside its body. This gives the robot the ability to hover in mid-air and to manoeuvre between buildings.

Looking Forward

Tiny Fliers   Micro Aerial Vehicles (MAVs) are tiny flying machines, often with wingspans of less than fifteen centimetres and weighing less than a hundred grams.

In the future, squadrons of these machines may fly together performing tasks such as traffic monitoring, police surveillance and search-and-rescue operations.

A robot helicopter hovers over a simulated dangerous chemicals spillage. It can photograph and provide important information on a spill without risking the lives of human rescue workers.

Pest Controllers

Japanese company Yamaha have produced a range of small robot helicopters which spray fields more efficiently than crop-dusting aircraft.

Yamaha's RMAX robot can spray thirty hectares per day, but fly closer to the ground and use much less pesticide. Apart from saving money, it means less harmful pesticide builds up in the soil or creeps into water supplies.

Another flying robot makes a novel pest controller at airports. Robofalcon, with its two-metre wingspan, looks like an oversized bird of prey and scares bird flocks from runways.

Diving puts people and machines under pressure. Deeper than seventy or eighty metres and humans have to be placed inside a protective diving suit or a submarine.

Robots make great underwater divers. They don't need large supplies of air and can be built to withstand great pressure. They can also travel for hours, even days, without surfacing.

RoboPike, a robotic fish, leaps out of the water. RoboPike has a series of flexible body parts, controlled by electric motors, allowing it to mimic the swimming actions of a real fish.

Looking Back

AUSS One of the first AUVs was the Advanced Unmanned Search System (AUSS). It took ten years to develop before its launch in 1983. The five-metre-long, torpedo-shaped robot had no manipulator arm and its heavy zinc battery packs took over twenty hours to recharge.

In 1992, the long-serving robot discovered the wreckage of a 1950s Douglas Skyraider aircraft.

ROVs and AUVs

There are two main types of underwater robot – ROVs and AUVs. ROV stands for Remotely Operated Vehicle. These machines are controlled by a human operator, usually from a ship to which the robot is linked by a cable.

AUV stands for Autonomous Underwater Vehicle. These robots can navigate by themselves, although they may be pre-programmed to patrol a certain area or dive to a certain depth.

In 2003, the British-built *Autosub* AUV was programmed to travel over a hundred kilometres underneath the ice shelves of Antarctica.

Surveying and Discovery

Underwater robots monitor the world's seas and oceans. They carry sensors that can measure water temperature, pollution and its effects on sea life.

When fitted with arms, grippers and other tools, some robots can help recover wrecked aircraft, ships and submarines. In 1999, the *Deep Drone* ROV helped recover the flight recorder from an EgyptAir airliner that crashed in the Atlantic Ocean.

Technology in Action

This ROV robot is collecting two-thousand-year-old jugs from the Mediterranean seabed.

The Deepest Dive Ever

Date: 24 March 1995. Location: Challenger Deep in the Pacific Ocean, the deepest place on Earth. The five-metre-long Kaiko robot travels deeper than any other robot, to a depth of 10,911 metres below sea level.

The robot uses its powerful manipulator arm to place a plaque on the ocean floor. It powers up its lights and cameras to photograph marine life before beginning its slow climb back to the surface.

A robotic arm extends from the Space Shuttle *Endeavor* as it docks with the International Space Station.

Robots are often used in space exploration to perform one-way missions, when they have no chance of returning to Earth.

Robotic probes have flown past, or landed on, the planets of our solar system. The vast distances involved, and the extreme conditions on other planets, mean that it is likely to remain easier to send machines rather than humans for many decades.

Exploring the Solar System

October 1998 saw the launch of the most intelligent spacecraft yet built: *Deep Space 1*. There were three AI systems on board, each with a different task:

● **The Autonomous Navigation System** steered the craft by comparing its position to well-known stars and asteroids.

● **The Remote Agent** was the spacecraft's "brain". It was programmed with a set of goals, but had freedom. If it spotted an interesting asteroid or comet, for example, *Deep Space 1* could stop what it was doing and investigate.

● **The Beacon Monitor** was its communication system, transmitting messages back to Earth, such as "Everything's fine", or "I need help now!".

Looking Back

Mars Milestone In 1976, the first-ever robots to visit Mars landed safely. The *Viking I* and *Viking II* landers sent back high-resolution photos of the Martian surface.

Unlike future roving robots, the two Vikings were unable to move. A simple robot arm collected rock and soil samples close to the robots. These samples were analyzed inside the machines.

Looking Forward

Robot Colonies Future Mars rovers are already being planned that will be able to adapt themselves to different kinds of terrain.

The ultimate aim is to send teams of robot rovers to work together on the Martian surface. They would build robot colonies, and lay the foundations for human visits and human bases.

Exploring The Red Planet

NASA's two Mars Exploration Rovers, *Spirit* and *Opportunity*, reached the red planet in January 2004. Over the course of their ninety-day mission the robots acted independently to navigate across part of Mars.

The robots travelled up to a hundred metres per day. They investigated the planet's rocks and found strong evidence that water may have once existed on Mars.

A Mars Exploration Rover. Cameras mounted on its mast provide panoramic views of Mars. The robot arm (bottom left) carries further cameras, sensors and a tool which can grind away the outer surface of a rock.

Robots can assist human surgeons in performing operations with incredible accuracy and without a hint of hand tremor. Some can drill pinpoint holes in bones. Others hold essential tools in place or transmit pictures from inside a patient's body.

Robots can help people with disabilities live a more normal life. A Japanese robot arm system called Myspoon helps people feed themselves without the aid of a nurse.

A human surgeon (bottom left) views an operation using 3D images while controlling the Da Vinci robot (centre) as a microsurgery operation is performed.

Virtual Reality Operations

Robots are enabling surgeons to operate without having to touch the patient. Working from a separate room, the surgeon operates by looking at a "virtual reality" image of the patient.

The movements of the surgeon's hands are transmitted from the gloves he is wearing to a manipulator in the operating theatre.

Cutting Across Continents

It is June 2000. A patient at a hospital in Rome is having surgery on his kidneys. However, the surgeon performing the operation is not in the room, or even in the country. He is in Baltimore, USA.

Through a combination of computers, telecommunication, cameras, and an advanced surgical robot, the surgeon is able to see, touch and manipulate as necessary in order to carry out a successful operation. Better still, the robot offers three-dimensional vision and a perfectly still hand.

Nursebots

Researchers are working on developing mobile personal service robots to help the elderly and other patients who need regular supervision. Working in nursing homes or in people's own houses, the robots would remind patients when to take their medication and can fetch and carry items for them.

Rehab Robots Patients recovering from major accidents and operations can require hundreds of hours of physiotherapy.

Researchers in the USA, Germany, Denmark and Japan are developing rehab robots that help patients exercise carefully. These robots will support a patient's body whilst directing them to move in the safest and most beneficial way to improve their health.

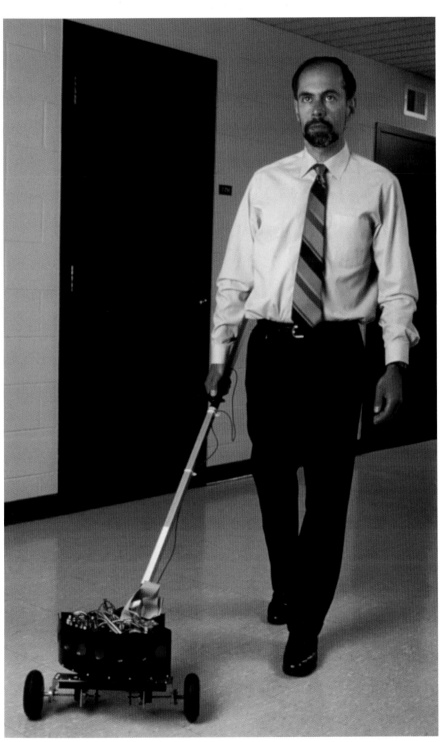

Nursebots would be programmed to detect emergency situations such as heart failure and be able to alert emergency services. Eventually these robots could even provide companionship for elderly people who are forced to live alone.

Guidecane, a robot guide for the blind, has a series of ultrasonic sensors that detect obstacles in its path. These are used to constantly update and recalculate the best route to take.

23

Today, robots are increasingly being used in military situations. Robots act as spies or security guards, or check out potential threats and traps.

Robotic rifles, controlled from a distance of up to a kilometre, are under development. As more military robots enter service, the prospect of robot-led conflicts thirty or forty years from now is not so far-fetched.

Robot Sentries

On the ground and under the water, robot sentries and security guards can patrol and keep watch with their sensors and camera systems. They can be stationed at the perimeters of a base or travel through the corridors of a building. Unlike human guards, robots remain alert and can work unceasingly for long shifts.

Robots In Iraq

A number of robots were deployed during the invasion of Iraq by US-led coalition forces in 2003. Some were land robots such as Packbot and Matilda, sent to check out areas for booby traps and other threats. Most were UAVs (see pages 16–17) used to spy on targets or enemy troop movements.

One unit of soldiers was about to land in a secret location in Iraq when a Predator flying robot alerted the unit to dangers on the ground. The mission was aborted, probably saving some of the soldiers' lives.

This mobile wheeled robot (right), fitted with a protective frame, is designed to be sent into danger areas and report back on potential threats without risking human soldiers' lives.

Robotic Assassination

3 November 2002. A Predator UAV flies over the Middle Eastern country of Yemen. It carries a deadly cargo – a Hellfire air-to-ground guided missile.

The robot flier is being controlled by a CIA pilot on the ground in the African nation of Djibouti. It homes in on its target – a vehicle carrying six members of the al-Qaeda terrorist group. The Predator releases the Hellfire missile, which destroys the vehicle and kills all those inside it.

The Raptor UAV is designed to fly over battlefields and provide early warning against short-range missiles fired by the enemy.

Looking Back

ROBART In the early 1980s, the American ROBART project produced the first robot security guards capable of working by themselves. ROBART 1 could only spot movement using its motion sensors. It could not assess whether the movement was a human intruder or not.

ROBART III, completed in 1993, was a vast improvement. The robot could detect and track an intruder.

A Japanese boy plays with his Sony AIBO robot dog. The AIBO mimics real dog actions such as barking and playing fetch and can also respond to its owner.

It is not all hard work for robots. Some provide people with great entertainment. Demonstration robots impress people at fairs and events, whilst the latest generation of home robots boast some amazing features.

Robot Pets and Toys

Robots at home are making excellent playmates. Many can speak and recognize hundreds or thousands of words, play games, make music and perform simple tasks.

Sony's AIBO robot dog is the best-selling home robot. It is capable of interacting with owners and displaying six different emotions.

Looking Back

Early Hobby Bots Heathkit's Hero-1 was a popular hobby robot of the early 1980s, despite costing over a thousand US dollars. Owners had to slowly build its fifteen circuit boards. The robot's arm could be programmed to lift objects, providing they weighed less than 440 grams.

The robot had just four kilobytes of memory. Today, a typical PC's hard disk has over five million times that memory space.

Sporting Robots

Fast-moving dynamic ball sports can make ideal test applications for serious robotics research. They require a robot's sensors, controller and movement systems to all work together quickly and accurately.

Toshiba have developed a two-armed robot which can play a simple game of volleyball, whilst the Dynamic Brain humanoid robot can juggle balls.

Robot Competitions

Dozens of competitions enable people to pit their robot-building and programming skills against others. Some are destructive robot combat competitions such as Battling Bots or Robot Wars, which first appeared in 1994. Others require robots to work together in a team to play a form of soccer in worldwide Robocup competitions.

Technology in Action

The Mighty Robosaurus

Towering over you, thirteen metres high, a mighty dinosaur-shaped robot breathes six-metre-long blasts of flame from its nostrils. The monster is called Robosaurus and it goes about its work, entertaining and amazing crowds at events.

Using its powerful hydraulic grippers, Robosaurus lifts cars, trucks and even old aircraft up to the height of a five-storey building. It then crushes them with over ten thousand kilograms of brutal force.

Robosaurus shoots giant flames from its nostrils. This entertainments robot weighs a hefty twenty-six tonnes.

The robot revolution has barely begun. Robots are in their infancy and many challenges lie ahead. No one can predict with certainty what future technology will bring, but advances are occurring every year.

The numbers of robots, the tasks they can perform, and their ability to assist people are all expected to increase massively. More and more robots are likely to serve in military and police forces and in hospitals, schools and offices.

Disarming landmines is tough, slow and dangerous work. In the future, flying mine-disposal robots may be able to clear land without risk.

Looking Back

Shakey Robots have made major strides forward since the arrival of the first robots in the 1960s. The first mobile robot was called Shakey and was the size of several people. Controlled by a computer that filled an entire room, the robot took around thirty minutes to move one metre.

Today's machines are far quicker and more powerful than Shakey. And they can be made small enough to sit in the palm of your hand.

Home Helpers

In the future it is likely that robots will perform a range of valuable tasks in the home. These multi-function machines will be able to play games, guard the house and educate children and adults.

They will be capable of communicating with smart appliances in the kitchen, and perform routine shopping and research tasks for their owners over the Internet.

Further And Faster

As robots become safer, more reliable and better at navigating, they will be built to travel and operate at faster speeds. Some may also travel to other galaxies across the universe.

Looking Forward

Nanobots Technology is shrinking. A nanometre is a billionth of a metre – the width of ten atoms. In the distant future, nanotechnology may be capable of building robots to this phenomenally small scale.

Their impact could be enormous. In medicine, nanobots could scrub blood vessels free of cholesterol and unblock clogged arteries and veins. Nanobots could inhabit materials and machinery, detecting wear and repairing damage.

Other space robots will land on and explore the planets and moons of our own solar system. Launched in March 2004, the Rosetta-Philae robot probe hopes to ride piggyback on a comet in 2014 after a journey of over seven billion kilometres.

An artist's impression of what a nanobot submarine, designed to travel through a human blood vessel, might look like. Such a robot may be capable of removing cholesterol and reducing the chances of heart disease.

1921 Playwright Karel Capek is the first to coin the term *robot* in his play *Rossum's Universal Robots*.

1938 The first programmable spray-painting machine is designed for the DeVilbiss Company.

1940s The first computers, including Colossus and ENIAC, are invented and used.

1948 *Cybernetics*, a book by MIT professor Norbert Weiner, is published. The book looks at how communications and control work in animals and might work in machines.

1950s Devol and Engelberger form the first company to develop and sell robots.

1959 The Artificial Intelligence Laboratory at MIT is founded.

1966 One of the very earliest mobile robots, Shakey, is invented.

1969 The first computer-controlled robot arm, driven by electric motors, called the Stanford Arm, is invented.

1975 The PUMA robot arm is invented. Versions of this arm and its technology become widely used in industry.

1976 The robot arms on the *Viking I* and *II* spacecraft become the first robots to work on the surface of another planet, Mars.

1979 The Stanford Cart is developed. It is an autonomous robotic vehicle that can navigate across a room full of obstacles.

1980s The WABOT and WABIAN series of humanoid robots are developed in Waseda University, Japan.

1986 The Remotely Operated Vehicle, *Jason Jr.*, photographs the inside of the wreck of the *Titanic.*

1988 The first Helpmate AGV starts work ferrying supplies around an American hospital.

1990 The Robodoc surgical assistant robot is invented and trialled.

1994 The Robot Wars competition is founded.

1997 The first RoboCup football competition is held.

1997 *Sojourner* becomes the first robot to move around on the surface of another planet when it reaches Mars.

1998 Work begins on MIT's groundbreaking Kismet robot.

1999 The Sony corporation release their first AIBO robotic dogs.

2001 The *Global Hawk* UAV travels over 13,000 km across the Pacific.

2002 Humanoid robots play football at RoboCup for the first time.

actuator A system or device, like an electric motor, which makes part or all of a robot move.

automata Mechanical devices that imitate the movements of a person or another living creature.

autonomous A machine that makes decisions and works by itself.

biped A two-legged creature or machine, such as a robot.

circuit board Boards containing electronic parts linked together.

compressed air system A way of moving a robot by using air in tubes to push its parts.

controller The part of the robot that makes decisions and instructs other parts of the robot.

degrees of freedom The different directions in which a robot can move.

feedback Information about the robot or its surroundings which are collected from sensors and sent to a robot's controller.

flight recorder A system housed in a tough box that records the speed, direction and other important details of an aircraft flight.

hydraulic pistons A piston is a sliding shaft which fits closely inside a tube called a cylinder. Hydraulic pistons are moved by liquid in a system to drive the parts of some robots.

hydraulics A power system using liquids in cylinders found in some robots.

humanoid A robot that looks like or acts in similar ways to people.

International Space Station A large spacecraft holding up to seven astronauts, which orbits Earth and is expected to be completed in 2006.

kilobyte A measure of computer memory. A regular floppy disk holds 1,440 kilobytes.

manipulator Another word for a robot gripper or tool that handles objects.

microprocessor A small computer built from one or a small number of silicon chips.

nanotechnology Technology created at an incredibly small scale measured in billionths of a metre.

prototype An experimental design of part or all of a machine for testing purposes.

radar A system which bounces radio waves off objects to work out how far away they are.

sensor A device that collects information about the robot or its surroundings.

smart appliance An electrical good, like a fridge or a microwave oven, which uses computer technology to communicate with other electronic items.

Space Shuttle A reusable American spacecraft which has flown over a hundred missions into space.

teleoperated Controlled from a distance by a human operator.

touchscreen A computer-controlled screen that not only displays information but can be pressed to select options and commands.

tranquillizer dart A small, pointed object covered with a drug, which causes creatures to go to sleep.

ultrasonic sensor A way of measuring distances using very high-pitched sounds.

virtual reality Computer systems which simulate real life in some way.

Further Information

Further Reading

Robots by Ruth Aylett (Barron's Educational, 2002)

Robotics: Intelligent Machines for the New Century by Ellen Thro (Facts on File, 2003)

How To Build Robots by Clive Gifford (Oxford University Press, 2001)

Twenty-First Century Debates: Artificial Intelligence by Alex Woolf (Hodder Wayland, 2002)

DVDs

Robots Rising (The Discovery Channel)

Robot Wars: Sir Killalot and the House Robots (International Licensing)

Let's Talk Robotics (Central Operation of Resources for Educators)

Websites

http://robots.net/
The site to head to for the latest news and hyperlinks in the world of robotics.

http://www.thetech.org/robotics/
A brilliant online museum that explains the workings of robots and includes a timeline and videos of some robots in action.

http://www.robocup.org/02.html
The official homepage of the world's biggest robot soccer competitions.

http://www.robotcafe.com/
An enormous collection of links to famous robot makers, robots, competitions and much more.

http://www.robosaurus.com/home.html
The official homepage of the mighty Robosaurus car-crushing entertainment dinosaur.